SQL Server Reportir
Complete Self-Asse:

The guidance in this Self-Assessment is based on SQL Server Reporting Services best practices and standards in business process architecture, design and quality management. The guidance is also based on the professional judgment of the individual collaborators listed in the Acknowledgments.

Notice of rights

Copyright © by The Art of Service
http://theartofservice.com
service@theartofservice.com

Table of Contents

About The Art of Service

The Art of Service, Business Process Architects since 2000, is dedicated to helping stakeholders achieve excellence.

Defining, designing, creating, and implementing a process to solve a stakeholders challenge or meet an objective is the most valuable role… In EVERY group, company, organization and department.

Unless you're talking a one-time, single-use project, there should be a process. Whether that process is managed and implemented by humans, AI, or a combination of the two, it needs to be designed by someone with a complex enough perspective to ask the right questions.

Someone capable of asking the right questions and step back and say, 'What are we really trying to accomplish here? And is there a different way to look at it?'

With The Art of Service's Standard Requirements Self-Assessments, we empower people who can do just that — whether their title is marketer, entrepreneur, manager, salesperson, consultant, Business Process Manager, executive assistant, IT Manager, CIO etc... —they are the people who rule the future. They are people who watch the process as it happens, and ask the right questions to make the process work better.

Contact us when you need any support with this Self-Assessment and any help with templates, blue-prints and examples of standard documents you might need:

http://theartofservice.com
service@theartofservice.com

Acknowledgments

This checklist was developed under the auspices of The Art of Service, chaired by Gerardus Blokdyk.

Representatives from several client companies participated in the preparation of this Self-Assessment.

Our deepest gratitude goes out to Matt Champagne, Ph.D. Surveys Expert, for his invaluable help and advise in structuring the Self Assessment.

Mr Champagne can be contacted at http://matthewchampagne.com/

In addition, we are thankful for the design and printing services provided.

Included Resources - how to access

Included with your purchase of the book is the SQL Server Reporting Services Self-Assessment Spreadsheet Dashboard which contains all questions and Self-Assessment areas and auto-generates insights, graphs, and project RACI planning - all with examples to get you started right away.

Get it now- you will be glad you did - do it now, before you forget.

How? Simply send an email to **access@theartofservice.com** with this books' title in the subject to get the SQL Server Reporting Services Self Assessment Tool right away.

Your feedback is invaluable to us

If you recently bought this book, we would love to hear from you! You can do this by writing a review on amazon (or the online store where you purchased this book) about your last purchase! As part of our continual service improvement process, we love to hear real client experiences and feedback.

How does it work?
To post a review on Amazon, just log in to your account and click on the Create Your Own Review button (under Customer Reviews) of the relevant product page. You can find examples of product reviews in Amazon. If you purchased from another online store, simply follow their procedures.

What happens when I submit my review?
Once you have submitted your review, send us an email at review@theartofservice.com with the link to your review so we can properly thank you for your feedback.

Purpose of this Self-Assessment

This Self-Assessment has been developed to improve understanding of the requirements and elements of SQL Server Reporting Services, based on best practices and standards in business process architecture, design and quality management.

It is designed to allow for a rapid Self-Assessment to determine how closely existing management practices and procedures correspond to the elements of the Self-Assessment.

The criteria of requirements and elements of SQL Server Reporting Services have been rephrased in the format of a Self-Assessment questionnaire, with a seven-criterion scoring system, as explained in this document.

In this format, even with limited background knowledge of SQL Server Reporting Services, a manager can quickly review existing operations to determine how they measure up to the standards. This in turn can serve as the starting point of a 'gap analysis' to identify management tools or system elements that might usefully be implemented in the organization to help improve overall performance.

How to use the Self-Assessment

On the following pages are a series of questions to identify to what extent your SQL Server Reporting Services initiative is complete in comparison to the requirements set in standards.

To facilitate answering the questions, there is a space in front of each question to enter a score on a scale of '1' to '5'.

1 Strongly Disagree

2 Disagree

3 Neutral

4 Agree

5 Strongly Agree

Read the question and rate it with the following in front of mind:

**'In my belief,
the answer to this question is clearly defined'.**

There are two ways in which you can choose to interpret this statement;
1. how aware are you that the answer to the question is clearly defined
2. for more in-depth analysis you can choose to gather evidence and confirm the answer to the question. This

obviously will take more time, most Self-Assessment users opt for the first way to interpret the question and dig deeper later on based on the outcome of the overall Self-Assessment.

A score of '1' would mean that the answer is not clear at all, where a '5' would mean the answer is crystal clear and defined. Leave emtpy when the question is not applicable or you don't want to answer it, you can skip it without affecting your score. Write your score in the space provided.

After you have responded to all the appropriate statements in each section, compute your average score for that section, using the formula provided, and round to the nearest tenth. Then transfer to the corresponding spoke in the SQL Server Reporting Services Scorecard on the second next page of the Self-Assessment.

Your completed SQL Server Reporting Services Scorecard will give you a clear presentation of which SQL Server Reporting Services areas need attention.

SQL Server Reporting Services Scorecard Example

Example of how the finalized Scorecard can look like:

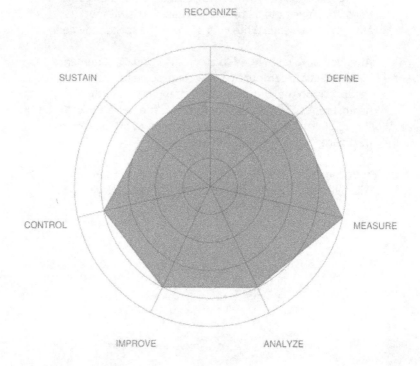

SQL Server Reporting Services Scorecard

Your Scores:

BEGINNING OF THE SELF-ASSESSMENT:

CRITERION #1: RECOGNIZE

INTENT: Be aware of the need for change. Recognize that there is an unfavorable variation, problem or symptom.

In my belief, the answer to this question is clearly defined:

5 Strongly Agree

4 Agree

3 Neutral

2 Disagree

1 Strongly Disagree

1. How do you prevent errors and rework?
<--- Score

2. How do we Identify specific SQL Server Reporting Services investment and emerging trends?
<--- Score

3. Is it clear when you think of the day ahead of you what activities and tasks you need to

complete?
<--- Score

4. Who needs to know about SQL Server Reporting Services ?
<--- Score

5. Who else hopes to benefit from it?
<--- Score

6. What vendors make products that address the SQL Server Reporting Services needs?
<--- Score

7. Does our organization need more SQL Server Reporting Services education?
<--- Score

8. What would happen if SQL Server Reporting Services weren't done?
<--- Score

9. What problems are you facing and how do you consider SQL Server Reporting Services will circumvent those obstacles?
<--- Score

10. What else needs to be measured?
<--- Score

11. Consider your own SQL Server Reporting Services project. what types of organizational problems do you think might be causing or affecting your problem, based on the work done so far?
<--- Score

12. What do we need to start doing?
<--- Score

13. Will new equipment/products be required to facilitate SQL Server Reporting Services delivery for example is new software needed?
<--- Score

14. Does SQL Server Reporting Services create potential expectations in other areas that need to be recognized and considered?
<--- Score

15. Why do we need to keep records?
<--- Score

16. What is the smallest subset of the problem we can usefully solve?
<--- Score

17. Who defines the rules in relation to any given issue?
<--- Score

18. Are there SQL Server Reporting Services problems defined?
<--- Score

19. How does it fit into our organizational needs and tasks?
<--- Score

20. When a SQL Server Reporting Services manager recognizes a problem, what options are available?

<--- Score

21. Have you identified your SQL Server Reporting Services key performance indicators?
<--- Score

22. How do you identify the kinds of information that you will need?
<--- Score

23. How are the SQL Server Reporting Services's objectives aligned to the organization's overall business strategy?
<--- Score

24. Will a response program recognize when a crisis occurs and provide some level of response?
<--- Score

25. Will SQL Server Reporting Services deliverables need to be tested and, if so, by whom?
<--- Score

26. How much are sponsors, customers, partners, stakeholders involved in SQL Server Reporting Services? In other words, what are the risks, if SQL Server Reporting Services does not deliver successfully?
<--- Score

27. Are there recognized SQL Server Reporting Services problems?
<--- Score

28. How are we going to measure success?
<--- Score

29. What are the business objectives to be achieved with SQL Server Reporting Services?
<--- Score

30. Can Management personnel recognize the monetary benefit of SQL Server Reporting Services?
<--- Score

31. What situation(s) led to this SQL Server Reporting Services Self Assessment?
<--- Score

32. Think about the people you identified for your SQL Server Reporting Services project and the project responsibilities you would assign to them. what kind of training do you think they would need to perform these responsibilities effectively?
<--- Score

33. What information do users need?
<--- Score

34. Are controls defined to recognize and contain problems?
<--- Score

35. Do we know what we need to know about this topic?
<--- Score

36. What tools and technologies are needed for a custom SQL Server Reporting Services project?
<--- Score

37. What should be considered when identifying

available resources, constraints, and deadlines?
<--- Score

38. Are there any specific expectations or concerns about the SQL Server Reporting Services team, SQL Server Reporting Services itself?
<--- Score

39. What training and capacity building actions are needed to implement proposed reforms?
<--- Score

40. As a sponsor, customer or management, how important is it to meet goals, objectives?
<--- Score

41. How do you identify the information basis for later specification of performance or acceptance criteria?
<--- Score

42. How can auditing be a preventative security measure?
<--- Score

43. What are the expected benefits of SQL Server Reporting Services to the business?
<--- Score

44. How do you assess your SQL Server Reporting Services workforce capability and capacity needs, including skills, competencies, and staffing levels?
<--- Score

45. What prevents me from making the changes I know will make me a more effective SQL Server

Reporting Services leader?
<--- Score

46. For your SQL Server Reporting Services project, identify and describe the business environment. is there more than one layer to the business environment?
<--- Score

47. Will it solve real problems?
<--- Score

48. Who had the original idea?
<--- Score

49. What does SQL Server Reporting Services success mean to the stakeholders?
<--- Score

Add up total points for this section:
_ _ _ _ _ = Total points for this section

Divided by: _ _ _ _ _ _ (number of statements answered) = _ _ _ _ _ _
Average score for this section

Transfer your score to the SQL Server Reporting Services Index at the beginning of the Self-Assessment.

CRITERION #2: DEFINE:

INTENT: Formulate the business problem. Define the problem, needs and objectives.

In my belief, the answer to this question is clearly defined:

5 Strongly Agree

4 Agree

3 Neutral

2 Disagree

1 Strongly Disagree

1. Has anyone else (internal or external to the organization) attempted to solve this problem or a similar one before? If so, what knowledge can be leveraged from these previous efforts?
<--- Score

2. How do you keep key subject matter experts in the loop?
<--- Score

18

3. Who are the SQL Server Reporting Services improvement team members, including Management Leads and Coaches?
<--- Score

4. What would be the goal or target for a SQL Server Reporting Services's improvement team?
<--- Score

5. How and when will the baselines be defined?
<--- Score

6. Has the direction changed at all during the course of SQL Server Reporting Services? If so, when did it change and why?
<--- Score

7. How would one define SQL Server Reporting Services leadership?
<--- Score

8. What are the boundaries of the scope? What is in bounds and what is not? What is the start point? What is the stop point?
<--- Score

9. Is there a completed SIPOC representation, describing the Suppliers, Inputs, Process, Outputs, and Customers?
<--- Score

10. Is data collected and displayed to better understand customer(s) critical needs and requirements.
<--- Score

11. Is SQL Server Reporting Services linked to key business goals and objectives?
<--- Score

12. How can the value of SQL Server Reporting Services be defined?
<--- Score

13. Are Required Metrics Defined?
<--- Score

14. Is the SQL Server Reporting Services scope manageable?
<--- Score

15. Have all of the relationships been defined properly?
<--- Score

16. What key business process output measure(s) does SQL Server Reporting Services leverage and how?
<--- Score

17. Has the improvement team collected the 'voice of the customer' (obtained feedback – qualitative and quantitative)?
<--- Score

18. Have specific policy objectives been defined?
<--- Score

19. How does the SQL Server Reporting Services manager ensure against scope creep?
<--- Score

20. Has everyone on the team, including the team leaders, been properly trained?
<--- Score

21. Is the team formed and are team leaders (Coaches and Management Leads) assigned?
<--- Score

22. What baselines are required to be defined and managed?
<--- Score

23. Is a fully trained team formed, supported, and committed to work on the SQL Server Reporting Services improvements?
<--- Score

24. Will team members regularly document their SQL Server Reporting Services work?
<--- Score

25. In what way can we redefine the criteria of choice in our category in our favor, as Method introduced style and design to cleaning and Virgin America returned glamor to flying?
<--- Score

26. Do the problem and goal statements meet the SMART criteria (specific, measurable, attainable, relevant, and time-bound)?
<--- Score

27. Are security/privacy roles and responsibilities formally defined?
<--- Score

28. Are team charters developed?
<--- Score

29. Is the improvement team aware of the different versions of a process: what they think it is vs. what it actually is vs. what it should be vs. what it could be?
<--- Score

30. Have the customer needs been translated into specific, measurable requirements? How?
<--- Score

31. Are business processes mapped?
<--- Score

32. What critical content must be communicated – who, what, when, where, and how?
<--- Score

33. What constraints exist that might impact the team?
<--- Score

34. How is the team tracking and documenting its work?
<--- Score

35. Does the team have regular meetings?
<--- Score

36. Are approval levels defined for contracts and supplements to contracts?
<--- Score

37. If substitutes have been appointed, have they been briefed on the SQL Server Reporting Services

goals and received regular communications as to the progress to date?

<--- Score

38. What organizational structure is required?

<--- Score

39. Are there any constraints known that bear on the ability to perform SQL Server Reporting Services work? How is the team addressing them?

<--- Score

40. What specifically is the problem? Where does it occur? When does it occur? What is its extent?

<--- Score

41. What tools and roadmaps did you use for getting through the Define phase?

<--- Score

42. Are accountability and ownership for SQL Server Reporting Services clearly defined?

<--- Score

43. Is there regularly 100% attendance at the team meetings? If not, have appointed substitutes attended to preserve cross-functionality and full representation?

<--- Score

44. Is SQL Server Reporting Services currently on schedule according to the plan?

<--- Score

45. Has a project plan, Gantt chart, or similar been developed/completed?

<--- Score

46. Is there a completed, verified, and validated high-level 'as is' (not 'should be' or 'could be') business process map?
<--- Score

47. Are customer(s) identified and segmented according to their different needs and requirements?
<--- Score

48. Is the team sponsored by a champion or business leader?
<--- Score

49. What defines Best in Class?
<--- Score

50. What is the minimum educational requirement for potential new hires?
<--- Score

51. Will team members perform SQL Server Reporting Services work when assigned and in a timely fashion?
<--- Score

52. Are roles and responsibilities formally defined?
<--- Score

53. Do we all define SQL Server Reporting Services in the same way?
<--- Score

54. Are customers identified and high impact areas defined?
<--- Score

55. How would you define the culture here?
<--- Score

56. Who defines (or who defined) the rules and roles?
<--- Score

57. Are there different segments of customers?
<--- Score

58. How will the SQL Server Reporting Services team and the organization measure complete success of SQL Server Reporting Services?
<--- Score

59. Has a high-level 'as is' process map been completed, verified and validated?
<--- Score

60. Is there a critical path to deliver SQL Server Reporting Services results?
<--- Score

61. Are improvement team members fully trained on SQL Server Reporting Services?
<--- Score

62. Are different versions of process maps needed to account for the different types of inputs?
<--- Score

63. How do senior leaders promote an environment that fosters and requires legal and ethical behavior?
<--- Score

64. What are the Roles and Responsibilities for each team member and its leadership? Where is this documented?
<--- Score

65. When are meeting minutes sent out? Who is on the distribution list?
<--- Score

66. Is full participation by members in regularly held team meetings guaranteed?
<--- Score

67. Is the team adequately staffed with the desired cross-functionality? If not, what additional resources are available to the team?
<--- Score

68. Have all basic functions of SQL Server Reporting Services been defined?
<--- Score

69. Has/have the customer(s) been identified?
<--- Score

70. What are the dynamics of the communication plan?
<--- Score

71. Are audit criteria, scope, frequency and methods defined?
<--- Score

72. Is the scope of SQL Server Reporting Services defined?
<--- Score

73. Is the current 'as is' process being followed? If not, what are the discrepancies?
<--- Score

74. How was the 'as is' process map developed, reviewed, verified and validated?
<--- Score

75. How often are the team meetings?
<--- Score

76. When was the SQL Server Reporting Services start date?
<--- Score

77. Is it clearly defined in and to your organization what you do?
<--- Score

78. Is the team equipped with available and reliable resources?
<--- Score

79. How will variation in the actual durations of each activity be dealt with to ensure that the expected SQL Server Reporting Services results are met?
<--- Score

80. Has the SQL Server Reporting Services work been fairly and/or equitably divided and delegated among team members who are qualified and capable to perform the work? Has everyone contributed?
<--- Score

81. Has a team charter been developed and

communicated?
<--- Score

82. What are the compelling business reasons for embarking on SQL Server Reporting Services?
<--- Score

83. Is there a SQL Server Reporting Services management charter, including business case, problem and goal statements, scope, milestones, roles and responsibilities, communication plan?
<--- Score

84. How did the SQL Server Reporting Services manager receive input to the development of a SQL Server Reporting Services improvement plan and the estimated completion dates/times of each activity?
<--- Score

85. What customer feedback methods were used to solicit their input?
<--- Score

86. Is SQL Server Reporting Services Required?
<--- Score

87. What are the rough order estimates on cost savings/opportunities that SQL Server Reporting Services brings?
<--- Score

88. When is the estimated completion date?
<--- Score

89. Are task requirements clearly defined?
<--- Score

90. In what way can we redefine the criteria of choice clients have in our category in our favor?
<--- Score

Add up total points for this section:
_____ = Total points for this section

Divided by: _____ (number of statements answered) = _____
Average score for this section

Transfer your score to the SQL Server Reporting Services Index at the beginning of the Self-Assessment.

CRITERION #3: MEASURE:

INTENT: Gather the correct data.
Measure the current performance and
evolution of the situation.

In my belief, the answer to this
question is clearly defined:

5 Strongly Agree

4 Agree

3 Neutral

2 Disagree

1 Strongly Disagree

1. Which customers can't participate in our market
because they lack skills, wealth, or convenient access
to existing solutions?
<--- Score

2. What charts has the team used to display the
components of variation in the process?
<--- Score

3. What measurements are possible, practicable and meaningful?
<--- Score

4. What are our key indicators that you will measure, analyze and track?
<--- Score

5. Which customers cant participate in our SQL Server Reporting Services domain because they lack skills, wealth, or convenient access to existing solutions?
<--- Score

6. Are we taking our company in the direction of better and revenue or cheaper and cost?
<--- Score

7. Is long term and short term variability accounted for?
<--- Score

8. What will be measured?
<--- Score

9. What about SQL Server Reporting Services Analysis of results?
<--- Score

10. What measurements are being captured?
<--- Score

11. What particular quality tools did the team find helpful in establishing measurements?
<--- Score

12. How will measures be used to manage and adapt?
<--- Score

13. Who should receive measurement reports ?
<--- Score

14. How can you measure SQL Server Reporting
Services in a systematic way?
<--- Score

15. Is the solution cost-effective?
<--- Score

16. Where is it measured?
<--- Score

17. Have changes been properly/adequately analyzed
for effect?
<--- Score

18. Is performance measured?
<--- Score

19. How is the value delivered by SQL Server
Reporting Services being measured?
<--- Score

20. Is data collection planned and executed?
<--- Score

21. Is key measure data collection planned
and executed, process variation displayed and
communicated and performance baselined?
<--- Score

22. Are priorities and opportunities deployed

to your suppliers, partners, and collaborators to ensure organizational alignment?

<--- Score

23. What key measures identified indicate the performance of the business process?

<--- Score

24. How do we do risk analysis of rare, cascading, catastrophic events?

<--- Score

25. What are my customers expectations and measures?

<--- Score

26. How Will We Measure Success?

<--- Score

27. Why should we expend time and effort to implement measurement?

<--- Score

28. Are high impact defects defined and identified in the business process?

<--- Score

29. What is an unallowable cost?

<--- Score

30. Are losses documented, analyzed, and remedial processes developed to prevent future losses?

<--- Score

31. What is the total cost related to deploying SQL Server Reporting Services, including any

consulting or professional services?
<--- Score

32. Is Process Variation Displayed/Communicated?
<--- Score

33. What are the uncertainties surrounding estimates of impact?
<--- Score

34. Is there a Performance Baseline?
<--- Score

35. When is Knowledge Management Measured?
<--- Score

36. How to measure variability?
<--- Score

37. What are measures?
<--- Score

38. Does SQL Server Reporting Services systematically track and analyze outcomes for accountability and quality improvement?
<--- Score

39. Was a data collection plan established?
<--- Score

40. Among the SQL Server Reporting Services product and service cost to be estimated, which is considered hardest to estimate?
<--- Score

41. How do senior leaders create a focus on action

to accomplish the organization s objectives and improve performance?

<--- Score

42. Are there measurements based on task performance?

<--- Score

43. What are your key SQL Server Reporting Services organizational performance measures, including key short and longer-term financial measures?

<--- Score

44. Are key measures identified and agreed upon?

<--- Score

45. Have all non-recommended alternatives been analyzed in sufficient detail?

<--- Score

46. Have the concerns of stakeholders to help identify and define potential barriers been obtained and analyzed?

<--- Score

47. How are you going to measure success?

<--- Score

48. How is Knowledge Management Measured?

<--- Score

49. How large is the gap between current performance and the customer-specified (goal) performance?

<--- Score

50. Are the measurements objective?
<--- Score

51. What are the types and number of measures to use?
<--- Score

52. How can we measure the performance?
<--- Score

53. What are the costs of reform?
<--- Score

54. Do we effectively measure and reward individual and team performance?
<--- Score

55. Do we aggressively reward and promote the people who have the biggest impact on creating excellent SQL Server Reporting Services services/ products?
<--- Score

56. How do we focus on what is right -not who is right?
<--- Score

57. What Relevant Entities could be measured?
<--- Score

58. Have you found any 'ground fruit' or 'low-hanging fruit' for immediate remedies to the gap in performance?
<--- Score

59. How are measurements made?

<--- Score

60. What potential environmental factors impact the SQL Server Reporting Services effort?

<--- Score

61. How will you measure your SQL Server Reporting Services effectiveness?

<--- Score

62. Why do the measurements/indicators matter?

<--- Score

63. Does SQL Server Reporting Services analysis show the relationships among important SQL Server Reporting Services factors?

<--- Score

64. What evidence is there and what is measured?

<--- Score

65. What should be measured?

<--- Score

66. Can we do SQL Server Reporting Services without complex (expensive) analysis?

<--- Score

67. Is a solid data collection plan established that includes measurement systems analysis?

<--- Score

68. What is the right balance of time and resources between investigation, analysis, and discussion and dissemination?

<--- Score

69. Is data collected on key measures that were identified?
<--- Score

70. How do you measure success?
<--- Score

71. How will your organization measure success?
<--- Score

72. Which methods and measures do you use to determine workforce engagement and workforce satisfaction?
<--- Score

73. Which Stakeholder Characteristics Are Analyzed?
<--- Score

74. Why Measure?
<--- Score

75. What has the team done to assure the stability and accuracy of the measurement process?
<--- Score

76. Does the SQL Server Reporting Services task fit the client's priorities?
<--- Score

77. How to measure lifecycle phases?
<--- Score

78. Meeting the challenge: are missed SQL Server Reporting Services opportunities costing us

money?
<--- Score

79. How will effects be measured?
<--- Score

80. Who participated in the data collection for measurements?
<--- Score

81. How frequently do you track SQL Server Reporting Services measures?
<--- Score

82. Are there any easy-to-implement alternatives to SQL Server Reporting Services? Sometimes other solutions are available that do not require the cost implications of a full-blown project?
<--- Score

83. What are the agreed upon definitions of the high impact areas, defect(s), unit(s), and opportunities that will figure into the process capability metrics?
<--- Score

84. Will We Aggregate Measures across Priorities?
<--- Score

85. Have the types of risks that may impact SQL Server Reporting Services been identified and analyzed?
<--- Score

86. How will success or failure be measured?
<--- Score

87. Do staff have the necessary skills to collect,

analyze, and report data?
<--- Score

88. How do you identify and analyze stakeholders and their interests?
<--- Score

89. Does the practice systematically track and analyze outcomes related for accountability and quality improvement?
<--- Score

90. What are the key input variables? What are the key process variables? What are the key output variables?
<--- Score

91. How is progress measured?
<--- Score

92. Why do measure/indicators matter?
<--- Score

93. Why identify and analyze stakeholders and their interests?
<--- Score

94. Are process variation components displayed/ communicated using suitable charts, graphs, plots?
<--- Score

95. What methods are feasible and acceptable to estimate the impact of reforms?
<--- Score

96. How frequently do we track measures?
<--- Score

97. Is this an issue for analysis or intuition?
<--- Score

98. Customer Measures: How Do Customers See Us?
<--- Score

99. Are you taking your company in the direction of better and revenue or cheaper and cost?
<--- Score

100. Are the units of measure consistent?
<--- Score

101. What is measured?
<--- Score

102. What data was collected (past, present, future/ongoing)?
<--- Score

103. Is it possible to estimate the impact of unanticipated complexity such as wrong or failed assumptions, feedback, etc. on proposed reforms?
<--- Score

104. What to measure and why?
<--- Score

105. Does SQL Server Reporting Services analysis isolate the fundamental causes of problems?
<--- Score

106. Can We Measure the Return on Analysis?
<--- Score

Add up total points for this section:
_____ = Total points for this section

Divided by: _____ (number of
statements answered) = _____
Average score for this section

Transfer your score to the SQL Server
Reporting Services Index at the
beginning of the Self-Assessment.

CRITERION #4: ANALYZE:

INTENT: Analyze causes, assumptions and hypotheses.

In my belief, the answer to this question is clearly defined:

5 Strongly Agree

4 Agree

3 Neutral

2 Disagree

1 Strongly Disagree

1. What are the disruptive SQL Server Reporting Services technologies that enable our organization to radically change our business processes?
<--- Score

2. Have any additional benefits been identified that will result from closing all or most of the gaps?
<--- Score

3. What tools were used to narrow the list of possible causes?
<--- Score

4. Were any designed experiments used to generate additional insight into the data analysis?
<--- Score

5. An organizationally feasible system request is one that considers the mission, goals and objectives of the organization. key questions are: is the solution request practical and will it solve a problem or take advantage of an opportunity to achieve company goals?
<--- Score

6. Do you, as a leader, bounce back quickly from setbacks?
<--- Score

7. Is the gap/opportunity displayed and communicated in financial terms?
<--- Score

8. What successful thing are we doing today that may be blinding us to new growth opportunities?
<--- Score

9. Have the problem and goal statements been updated to reflect the additional knowledge gained from the analyze phase?
<--- Score

10. What are your current levels and trends in key measures or indicators of SQL Server Reporting Services product and process performance

that are important to and directly serve your customers? how do these results compare with the performance of your competitors and other organizations with similar offerings?
<--- Score

11. What were the financial benefits resulting from any 'ground fruit or low-hanging fruit' (quick fixes)?
<--- Score

12. What are our SQL Server Reporting Services Processes?
<--- Score

13. What other jobs or tasks affect the performance of the steps in the SQL Server Reporting Services process?
<--- Score

14. Can we add value to the current SQL Server Reporting Services decision-making process (largely qualitative) by incorporating uncertainty modeling (more quantitative)?
<--- Score

15. How was the detailed process map generated, verified, and validated?
<--- Score

16. Identify an operational issue in your organization. for example, could a particular task be done more quickly or more efficiently?
<--- Score

17. When conducting a business process reengineering study, what should we look for

when trying to identify business processes to change?
<--- Score

18. What is the cost of poor quality as supported by the team's analysis?
<--- Score

19. Was a detailed process map created to amplify critical steps of the 'as is' business process?
<--- Score

20. Think about some of the processes you undertake within your organization. which do you own?
<--- Score

21. What does the data say about the performance of the business process?
<--- Score

22. What controls do we have in place to protect data?
<--- Score

23. Is the SQL Server Reporting Services process severely broken such that a re-design is necessary?
<--- Score

24. What process should we select for improvement?
<--- Score

25. What quality tools were used to get through the analyze phase?
<--- Score

26. Do your employees have the opportunity to do

what they do best everyday?

<--- Score

27. What are your current levels and trends in key SQL Server Reporting Services measures or indicators of product and process performance that are important to and directly serve your customers?

<--- Score

28. Are gaps between current performance and the goal performance identified?

<--- Score

29. How is the way you as the leader think and process information affecting your organizational culture?

<--- Score

30. What did the team gain from developing a sub-process map?

<--- Score

31. Did any value-added analysis or 'lean thinking' take place to identify some of the gaps shown on the 'as is' process map?

<--- Score

32. Is the suppliers process defined and controlled?

<--- Score

33. How do mission and objectives affect the SQL Server Reporting Services processes of our organization?

<--- Score

34. What tools were used to generate the list of possible causes?
<--- Score

35. A compounding model resolution with available relevant data can often provide insight towards a solution methodology; which SQL Server Reporting Services models, tools and techniques are necessary?
<--- Score

36. Do our leaders quickly bounce back from setbacks?
<--- Score

37. What are the best opportunities for value improvement?
<--- Score

38. Did any additional data need to be collected?
<--- Score

39. What other organizational variables, such as reward systems or communication systems, affect the performance of this SQL Server Reporting Services process?
<--- Score

40. Is Data and process analysis, root cause analysis and quantifying the gap/opportunity in place?
<--- Score

41. Is the performance gap determined?
<--- Score

42. Think about the functions involved in your SQL

Server Reporting Services project. what processes flow from these functions?
<--- Score

43. What are the revised rough estimates of the financial savings/opportunity for SQL Server Reporting Services improvements?
<--- Score

44. Where is the data coming from to measure compliance?
<--- Score

45. Was a cause-and-effect diagram used to explore the different types of causes (or sources of variation)?
<--- Score

46. Were there any improvement opportunities identified from the process analysis?
<--- Score

47. Were Pareto charts (or similar) used to portray the 'heavy hitters' (or key sources of variation)?
<--- Score

48. What were the crucial 'moments of truth' on the process map?
<--- Score

49. How do you use SQL Server Reporting Services data and information to support organizational decision making and innovation?
<--- Score

50. How does the organization define, manage, and improve its SQL Server Reporting Services processes?

<--- Score

51. How do you measure the Operational performance of your key work systems and processes, including productivity, cycle time, and other appropriate measures of process effectiveness, efficiency, and innovation?
<--- Score

52. How do we promote understanding that opportunity for improvement is not criticism of the status quo, or the people who created the status quo?
<--- Score

53. Record-keeping requirements flow from the records needed as inputs, outputs, controls and for transformation of a SQL Server Reporting Services process. ask yourself: are the records needed as inputs to the SQL Server Reporting Services process available?
<--- Score

54. What conclusions were drawn from the team's data collection and analysis? How did the team reach these conclusions?
<--- Score

55. How often will data be collected for measures?
<--- Score

Add up total points for this section:
_ _ _ _ _ = Total points for this section

Divided by: _ _ _ _ _ _ (number of statements answered) = _ _ _ _ _ _

Average score for this section

Transfer your score to the SQL Server
Reporting Services Index at the
beginning of the Self-Assessment.

CRITERION #5: IMPROVE:

INTENT: Develop a practical solution. Innovate, establish and test the solution and to measure the results.

In my belief, the answer to this question is clearly defined:

5 Strongly Agree

4 Agree

3 Neutral

2 Disagree

1 Strongly Disagree

1. How will the organization know that the solution worked?
<--- Score

2. What communications are necessary to support the implementation of the solution?
<--- Score

3. Risk factors: what are the characteristics of SQL

Server Reporting Services that make it risky?

<--- Score

4. Is the solution technically practical?

<--- Score

5. Why improve in the first place?

<--- Score

6. Who will be responsible for documenting the SQL Server Reporting Services requirements in detail?

<--- Score

7. How do you improve your likelihood of success ?

<--- Score

8. How do the SQL Server Reporting Services results compare with the performance of your competitors and other organizations with similar offerings?

<--- Score

9. How significant is the improvement in the eyes of the end user?

<--- Score

10. What went well, what should change, what can improve?

<--- Score

11. What tools were most useful during the improve phase?

<--- Score

12. How will we know that a change is improvement?

<--- Score

13. What is the magnitude of the improvements?
<--- Score

14. What can we do to improve?
<--- Score

15. Risk events: what are the things that could go wrong?
<--- Score

16. What to do with the results or outcomes of measurements?
<--- Score

17. Is there a cost/benefit analysis of optimal solution(s)?
<--- Score

18. Is the implementation plan designed?
<--- Score

19. To what extent does management recognize SQL Server Reporting Services as a tool to increase the results?
<--- Score

20. Are we Assessing SQL Server Reporting Services and Risk?
<--- Score

21. Who controls the risk?
<--- Score

22. Can the solution be designed and implemented within an acceptable time period?

<--- Score

23. Are possible solutions generated and tested?
<--- Score

24. What error proofing will be done to address some of the discrepancies observed in the 'as is' process?
<--- Score

25. What actually has to improve and by how much?
<--- Score

26. What is the implementation plan?
<--- Score

27. For estimation problems, how do you develop an estimation statement?
<--- Score

28. What were the underlying assumptions on the cost-benefit analysis?
<--- Score

29. Who controls key decisions that will be made?
<--- Score

30. How did the team generate the list of possible solutions?
<--- Score

31. What needs improvement?
<--- Score

32. Who are the people involved in developing and implementing SQL Server Reporting Services?

<--- Score

33. How do you use other indicators, such as workforce retention, absenteeism, grievances, safety, and productivity, to assess and improve workforce engagement?
<--- Score

34. How important is the completion of a recognized college or graduate-level degree program in the hiring decision?
<--- Score

35. How can we improve SQL Server Reporting Services?
<--- Score

36. Does the goal represent a desired result that can be measured?
<--- Score

37. Is pilot data collected and analyzed?
<--- Score

38. How can we improve performance?
<--- Score

39. What do we want to improve?
<--- Score

40. For decision problems, how do you develop a decision statement?
<--- Score

41. How do we go about Comparing SQL Server Reporting Services approaches/solutions?

<--- Score

42. Is there a high likelihood that any recommendations will achieve their intended results?
<--- Score

43. At what point will vulnerability assessments be performed once SQL Server Reporting Services is put into production (e.g., ongoing Risk Management after implementation)?
<--- Score

44. Were any criteria developed to assist the team in testing and evaluating potential solutions?
<--- Score

45. How will you know that you have improved?
<--- Score

46. In the past few months, what is the smallest change we have made that has had the biggest positive result? What was it about that small change that produced the large return?
<--- Score

47. How do we measure improved SQL Server Reporting Services service perception, and satisfaction?
<--- Score

48. What are the implications of this decision 10 minutes, 10 months, and 10 years from now?
<--- Score

49. What improvements have been achieved?

<--- Score

50. Is Supporting SQL Server Reporting Services documentation required?
<--- Score

51. Is a solution implementation plan established, including schedule/work breakdown structure, resources, risk management plan, cost/budget, and control plan?
<--- Score

52. What tools were used to evaluate the potential solutions?
<--- Score

53. Was a pilot designed for the proposed solution(s)?
<--- Score

54. What evaluation strategy is needed and what needs to be done to assure its implementation and use?
<--- Score

55. How does the solution remove the key sources of issues discovered in the analyze phase?
<--- Score

56. How will you know when its improved?
<--- Score

57. If you could go back in time five years, what decision would you make differently? What is your best guess as to what decision you're making today you might regret five years from now?
<--- Score

58. How do we keep improving SQL Server Reporting Services?
<--- Score

59. Is the measure understandable to a variety of people?
<--- Score

60. Is there a small-scale pilot for proposed improvement(s)? What conclusions were drawn from the outcomes of a pilot?
<--- Score

61. Who will be using the results of the measurement activities?
<--- Score

62. How do we Improve SQL Server Reporting Services service perception, and satisfaction?
<--- Score

63. How do you measure progress and evaluate training effectiveness?
<--- Score

64. What is the risk?
<--- Score

65. How do we measure risk?
<--- Score

66. What is SQL Server Reporting Services's impact on utilizing the best solution(s)?
<--- Score

67. What attendant changes will need to be made to ensure that the solution is successful?
<--- Score

68. What is the team's contingency plan for potential problems occurring in implementation?
<--- Score

69. How do you improve workforce health, safety, and security? What are your performance measures and improvement goals for each of these workforce needs and what are any significant differences in these factors and performance measures or targets for different workplace environments?
<--- Score

70. Are there any constraints (technical, political, cultural, or otherwise) that would inhibit certain solutions?
<--- Score

71. How will the team or the process owner(s) monitor the implementation plan to see that it is working as intended?
<--- Score

72. Is the optimal solution selected based on testing and analysis?
<--- Score

73. How do we decide how much to remunerate an employee?
<--- Score

74. How do we improve productivity?

<--- Score

75. What should a proof of concept or pilot accomplish?
<--- Score

76. Are new and improved process ('should be') maps developed?
<--- Score

77. Who will be responsible for making the decisions to include or exclude requested changes once SQL Server Reporting Services is underway?
<--- Score

78. How to Improve?
<--- Score

79. What lessons, if any, from a pilot were incorporated into the design of the full-scale solution?
<--- Score

80. Are improved process ('should be') maps modified based on pilot data and analysis?
<--- Score

81. How Do We Link Measurement and Risk?
<--- Score

82. Do we cover the five essential competencies-Communication, Collaboration,Innovation, Adaptability, and Leadership that improve an organization's ability to leverage the new SQL Server Reporting Services in a volatile global economy?
<--- Score

83. How can skill-level changes improve SQL Server Reporting Services?
<--- Score

84. Are the best solutions selected?
<--- Score

85. What tools were used to tap into the creativity and encourage 'outside the box' thinking?
<--- Score

86. What resources are required for the improvement effort?
<--- Score

87. Describe the design of the pilot and what tests were conducted, if any?
<--- Score

88. How will you measure the results?
<--- Score

89. Is a contingency plan established?
<--- Score

90. What does the 'should be' process map/design look like?
<--- Score

91. Do we get business results?
<--- Score

92. How does the team improve its work?
<--- Score

Add up total points for this section:

_____ = Total points for this section

Divided by: _____ (number of statements answered) = _____
Average score for this section

Transfer your score to the SQL Server Reporting Services Index at the beginning of the Self-Assessment.

CRITERION #6: CONTROL:

INTENT: Implement the practical solution. Maintain the performance and correct possible complications.

In my belief, the answer to this question is clearly defined:

5 Strongly Agree

4 Agree

3 Neutral

2 Disagree

1 Strongly Disagree

1. Who has control over resources?
<--- Score

2. Is there a transfer of ownership and knowledge to process owner and process team tasked with the responsibilities.
<--- Score

3. What do we stand for--and what are we against?

<--- Score

4. Is there a recommended audit plan for routine surveillance inspections of SQL Server Reporting Services's gains?
<--- Score

5. Has the improved process and its steps been standardized?
<--- Score

6. Are operating procedures consistent?
<--- Score

7. What quality tools were useful in the control phase?
<--- Score

8. How might the organization capture best practices and lessons learned so as to leverage improvements across the business?
<--- Score

9. Implementation Planning- is a pilot needed to test the changes before a full roll out occurs?
<--- Score

10. What are the known security controls?
<--- Score

11. Who will be in control?
<--- Score

12. How will input, process, and output variables be checked to detect for sub-optimal conditions?
<--- Score

13. How likely is the current SQL Server Reporting Services plan to come in on schedule or on budget?

<--- Score

14. Were the planned controls working?

<--- Score

15. Is a response plan in place for when the input, process, or output measures indicate an 'out-of-control' condition?

<--- Score

16. What is the control/monitoring plan?

<--- Score

17. Who controls critical resources?

<--- Score

18. What is our theory of human motivation, and how does our compensation plan fit with that view?

<--- Score

19. How does your workforce performance management system support high-performance work and workforce engagement; consider workforce compensation, reward, recognition, and incentive practices; and reinforce a customer and business focus and achievement of your action plans?

<--- Score

20. How can we best use all of our knowledge repositories to enhance learning and sharing?

<--- Score

21. How will report readings be checked to effectively monitor performance?
<--- Score

22. Is knowledge gained on process shared and institutionalized?
<--- Score

23. How will the process owner verify improvement in present and future sigma levels, process capabilities?
<--- Score

24. Where do ideas that reach policy makers and planners as proposals for SQL Server Reporting Services strengthening and reform actually originate?
<--- Score

25. Are new process steps, standards, and documentation ingrained into normal operations?
<--- Score

26. Does a troubleshooting guide exist or is it needed?
<--- Score

27. How will the process owner and team be able to hold the gains?
<--- Score

28. How do our controls stack up?
<--- Score

29. What is your theory of human motivation, and how does your compensation plan fit with that view?
<--- Score

30. What should we measure to verify effectiveness gains?
<--- Score

31. Are suggested corrective/restorative actions indicated on the response plan for known causes to problems that might surface?
<--- Score

32. Whats the best design framework for SQL Server Reporting Services organization now that, in a post industrial-age if the top-down, command and control model is no longer relevant?
<--- Score

33. Have new or revised work instructions resulted?
<--- Score

34. Is new knowledge gained imbedded in the response plan?
<--- Score

35. How will the day-to-day responsibilities for monitoring and continual improvement be transferred from the improvement team to the process owner?
<--- Score

36. What other areas of the organization might benefit from the SQL Server Reporting Services team's improvements, knowledge, and learning?
<--- Score

37. Against what alternative is success being measured?

<--- Score

38. Are there documented procedures?
<--- Score

39. Does the SQL Server Reporting Services performance meet the customer's requirements?
<--- Score

40. Are documented procedures clear and easy to follow for the operators?
<--- Score

41. What are we attempting to measure/monitor?
<--- Score

42. What are the critical parameters to watch?
<--- Score

43. How do you encourage people to take control and responsibility?
<--- Score

44. If there currently is no plan, will a plan be developed?
<--- Score

45. What are the key elements of your SQL Server Reporting Services performance improvement system, including your evaluation, organizational learning, and innovation processes?
<--- Score

46. What is your quality control system?
<--- Score

47. Is a response plan established and deployed?
<--- Score

48. Is there a control plan in place for sustaining improvements (short and long-term)?
<--- Score

49. Will any special training be provided for results interpretation?
<--- Score

50. Is reporting being used or needed?
<--- Score

51. Does the response plan contain a definite closed loop continual improvement scheme (e.g., plan-do-check-act)?
<--- Score

52. Do the SQL Server Reporting Services decisions we make today help people and the planet tomorrow?
<--- Score

53. Are pertinent alerts monitored, analyzed and distributed to appropriate personnel?
<--- Score

54. What other systems, operations, processes, and infrastructures (hiring practices, staffing, training, incentives/rewards, metrics/dashboards/scorecards, etc.) need updates, additions, changes, or deletions in order to facilitate knowledge transfer and improvements?
<--- Score

55. Do you monitor the effectiveness of your SQL Server Reporting Services activities?
<--- Score

56. Is there a standardized process?
<--- Score

57. What key inputs and outputs are being measured on an ongoing basis?
<--- Score

58. Will existing staff require re-training, for example, to learn new business processes?
<--- Score

59. Do we monitor the SQL Server Reporting Services decisions made and fine tune them as they evolve?
<--- Score

60. How do controls support value?
<--- Score

61. What should the next improvement project be that is related to SQL Server Reporting Services?
<--- Score

62. Is there documentation that will support the successful operation of the improvement?
<--- Score

63. Who is the SQL Server Reporting Services process owner?
<--- Score

64. Why is change control necessary?

<--- Score

65. Does job training on the documented procedures need to be part of the process team's education and training?
<--- Score

66. What should we measure to verify efficiency gains?
<--- Score

67. How will new or emerging customer needs/requirements be checked/communicated to orient the process toward meeting the new specifications and continually reducing variation?
<--- Score

68. Does SQL Server Reporting Services appropriately measure and monitor risk?
<--- Score

69. Do the decisions we make today help people and the planet tomorrow?
<--- Score

70. What is the recommended frequency of auditing?
<--- Score

71. What can you control?
<--- Score

72. Are controls in place and consistently applied?
<--- Score

73. Were the planned controls in place?
<--- Score

74. What are your results for key measures or indicators of the accomplishment of your SQL Server Reporting Services strategy and action plans, including building and strengthening core competencies?

<--- Score

75. Is there a documented and implemented monitoring plan?

<--- Score

76. How do we enable market innovation while controlling security and privacy?

<--- Score

77. In the case of a SQL Server Reporting Services project, the criteria for the audit derive from implementation objectives. an audit of a SQL Server Reporting Services project involves assessing whether the recommendations outlined for implementation have been met. in other words, can we track that any SQL Server Reporting Services project is implemented as planned, and is it working?

<--- Score

78. Is there a SQL Server Reporting Services Communication plan covering who needs to get what information when?

<--- Score

Add up total points for this section:
_ _ _ _ _ = Total points for this section

Divided by: _ _ _ _ _ _ (number of

statements answered) = _____
Average score for this section

Transfer your score to the SQL Server
Reporting Services Index at the
beginning of the Self-Assessment.

CRITERION #7: SUSTAIN:

INTENT: Retain the benefits.

In my belief, the answer to this question is clearly defined:

5 Strongly Agree

4 Agree

3 Neutral

2 Disagree

1 Strongly Disagree

1. Will it be accepted by users?
<--- Score

2. How do you govern and fulfill your societal responsibilities?
<--- Score

3. What is something you believe that nearly no one agrees with you on?
<--- Score

4. How do we maintain SQL Server Reporting Services's Integrity?
<--- Score

5. Whose voice (department, ethnic group, women, older workers, etc) might you have missed hearing from in your company, and how might you amplify this voice to create positive momentum for your business?
<--- Score

6. What is the range of capabilities?
<--- Score

7. Who, on the executive team or the board, has spoken to a customer recently?
<--- Score

8. What counts that we are not counting?
<--- Score

9. If you were responsible for initiating and implementing major changes in your organization, what steps might you take to ensure acceptance of those changes?
<--- Score

10. What will be the consequences to the stakeholder (financial, reputation etc) if SQL Server Reporting Services does not go ahead or fails to deliver the objectives?
<--- Score

11. Have highly satisfied employees?
<--- Score

12. How Do We Create Buy-in?
<--- Score

13. How likely is it that a customer would recommend our company to a friend or colleague?
<--- Score

14. What are the gaps in my knowledge and experience?
<--- Score

15. Political -is anyone trying to undermine this project?
<--- Score

16. Legal and contractual - are we allowed to do this?
<--- Score

17. What threat is SQL Server Reporting Services addressing?
<--- Score

18. Who Uses What?
<--- Score

19. How do we manage SQL Server Reporting Services Knowledge Management (KM)?
<--- Score

20. You may have created your customer policies at a time when you lacked resources, technology wasn't up-to-snuff, or low service levels were the industry norm. Have those circumstances changed?
<--- Score

21. Will I get fired?
<--- Score

22. Who are the key stakeholders?
<--- Score

23. How do we make it meaningful in connecting SQL Server Reporting Services with what users do day-to-day?
<--- Score

24. What are the short and long-term SQL Server Reporting Services goals?
<--- Score

25. How can you negotiate SQL Server Reporting Services successfully with a stubborn boss, an irate client, or a deceitful coworker?
<--- Score

26. How would our PR, marketing, and social media change if we did not use outside agencies?
<--- Score

27. Is the impact that SQL Server Reporting Services has shown?
<--- Score

28. How do we foster innovation?
<--- Score

29. Are assumptions made in SQL Server Reporting Services stated explicitly?
<--- Score

30. Do you see more potential in people than they do in themselves?
<--- Score

31. What happens at this company when people fail?
<--- Score

32. What is the mission of the organization?
<--- Score

33. Think about the kind of project structure that would be appropriate for your SQL Server Reporting Services project. should it be formal and complex, or can it be less formal and relatively simple?
<--- Score

34. How Do We Know if We Are Successful?
<--- Score

35. What new services of functionality will be implemented next with SQL Server Reporting Services ?
<--- Score

36. What trouble can we get into?
<--- Score

37. Are we making progress (as leaders)?
<--- Score

38. Who do we want our customers to become?
<--- Score

39. What will drive SQL Server Reporting Services change?

<--- Score

40. What management system can we use to leverage the SQL Server Reporting Services experience, ideas, and concerns of the people closest to the work to be done?
<--- Score

41. Who are our customers?
<--- Score

42. What is our question?
<--- Score

43. What external factors influence our success?
<--- Score

44. Who will manage the integration of tools?
<--- Score

45. How much contingency will be available in the budget?
<--- Score

46. How will we know if we have been successful?
<--- Score

47. If we do not follow, then how to lead?
<--- Score

48. If you had to rebuild your organization without any traditional competitive advantages (i.e., no killer a technology, promising research, innovative product/service delivery model, etc.), how would your people have to approach their work and collaborate together in order to create the

necessary conditions for success?
<--- Score

49. Marketing budgets are tighter, consumers are more skeptical, and social media has changed forever the way we talk about SQL Server Reporting Services. How do we gain traction?
<--- Score

50. What are all of our SQL Server Reporting Services domains and what do they do?
<--- Score

51. Why should we adopt a SQL Server Reporting Services framework?
<--- Score

52. Among our stronger employees, how many see themselves at the company in three years? How many would leave for a 10 percent raise from another company?
<--- Score

53. How do we keep the momentum going?
<--- Score

54. Are we / should we be Revolutionary or evolutionary?
<--- Score

55. What is our competitive advantage?
<--- Score

56. Why should people listen to you?
<--- Score

57. Do we have the right capabilities and capacities?

<--- Score

58. How do we foster the skills, knowledge, talents, attributes, and characteristics we want to have?

<--- Score

59. Is maximizing SQL Server Reporting Services protection the same as minimizing SQL Server Reporting Services loss?

<--- Score

60. What are the challenges?

<--- Score

61. Who is On the Team?

<--- Score

62. Do we have the right people on the bus?

<--- Score

63. Which criteria are used to determine which projects are going to be pursued or discarded?

<--- Score

64. How long will it take to change?

<--- Score

65. Do we say no to customers for no reason?

<--- Score

66. Can we maintain our growth without detracting from the factors that have contributed to our success?

<--- Score

67. What trophy do we want on our mantle?
<--- Score

68. How do we engage the workforce, in addition to satisfying them?
<--- Score

69. In the past year, what have you done (or could you have done) to increase the accurate perception of this company/brand as ethical and honest?
<--- Score

70. What are we challenging, in the sense that Mac challenged the PC or Dove tackled the Beauty Myth?
<--- Score

71. Who is going to care?
<--- Score

72. What principles do we value?
<--- Score

73. Are you satisfied with your current role? If not, what is missing from it?
<--- Score

74. How do we Lead with SQL Server Reporting Services in Mind?
<--- Score

75. Do you have any supplemental information to add to this checklist?
<--- Score

76. What is performance excellence?
<--- Score

77. Have benefits been optimized with all key stakeholders?
<--- Score

78. Why are SQL Server Reporting Services skills important?
<--- Score

79. How do senior leaders deploy your organizations vision and values through your leadership system, to the workforce, to key suppliers and partners, and to customers and other stakeholders, as appropriate?
<--- Score

80. Why don't our customers like us?
<--- Score

81. What did we miss in the interview for the worst hire we ever made?
<--- Score

82. Do you have an implicit bias for capital investments over people investments?
<--- Score

83. Who are you going to put out of business, and why?
<--- Score

84. We picked a method, now what?
<--- Score

85. Schedule -can it be done in the given time?
<--- Score

86. Are we making progress?
<--- Score

87. In retrospect, of the projects that we pulled the plug on, what percent do we wish had been allowed to keep going, and what percent do we wish had ended earlier?
<--- Score

88. Is there any reason to believe the opposite of my current belief?
<--- Score

89. What are our long-range and short-range goals?
<--- Score

90. How do you determine the key elements that affect SQL Server Reporting Services workforce satisfaction? how are these elements determined for different workforce groups and segments?
<--- Score

91. When information truly is ubiquitous, when reach and connectivity are completely global, when computing resources are infinite, and when a whole new set of impossibilities are not only possible, but happening, what will that do to our business?
<--- Score

92. Which models, tools and techniques are necessary?
<--- Score

93. What current systems have to be understood and/or changed?
<--- Score

94. Are the criteria for selecting recommendations stated?
<--- Score

95. How can we become the company that would put us out of business?
<--- Score

96. What do we do when new problems arise?
<--- Score

97. What is a good product?
<--- Score

98. Do we think we know, or do we know we know ?
<--- Score

99. Were lessons learned captured and communicated?
<--- Score

100. Is our strategy driving our strategy? Or is the way in which we allocate resources driving our strategy?
<--- Score

101. What is our mission?
<--- Score

102. In what ways are SQL Server Reporting Services vendors and us interacting to ensure safe

and effective use?
<--- Score

103. Who will be responsible for deciding whether SQL Server Reporting Services goes ahead or not after the initial investigations?
<--- Score

104. Have new benefits been realized?
<--- Score

105. Are we paying enough attention to the partners our company depends on to succeed?
<--- Score

106. What would have to be true for the option on the table to be the best possible choice?
<--- Score

107. Who sets the SQL Server Reporting Services standards?
<--- Score

108. Do you keep 50% of your time unscheduled?
<--- Score

109. Where can we break convention?
<--- Score

110. What are specific SQL Server Reporting Services Rules to follow?
<--- Score

111. Do I know what I'm doing? And who do I call if I don't?
<--- Score

112. Are we relevant? Will we be relevant five years from now? Ten?
<--- Score

113. If we weren't already in this business, would we enter it today? And if not, what are we going to do about it?
<--- Score

114. What role does communication play in the success or failure of a SQL Server Reporting Services project?
<--- Score

115. What am I trying to prove to myself, and how might it be hijacking my life and business success?
<--- Score

116. Who are four people whose careers I've enhanced?
<--- Score

117. Is there any existing SQL Server Reporting Services governance structure?
<--- Score

118. What are the critical success factors?
<--- Score

119. How do we ensure that implementations of SQL Server Reporting Services products are done in a way that ensures safety?
<--- Score

120. What are the business goals SQL Server

Reporting Services is aiming to achieve?
<--- Score

121. How do we accomplish our long range SQL Server Reporting Services goals?
<--- Score

122. What information is critical to our organization that our executives are ignoring?
<--- Score

123. Are there SQL Server Reporting Services Models?
<--- Score

124. Has the investment re-baselined during the past fiscal year?
<--- Score

125. How will we ensure we get what we expected?
<--- Score

126. How important is SQL Server Reporting Services to the user organizations mission?
<--- Score

127. How to deal with SQL Server Reporting Services Changes?
<--- Score

128. What business benefits will SQL Server Reporting Services goals deliver if achieved?
<--- Score

129. What is Tricky About This?
<--- Score

130. What stupid rule would we most like to kill?
<--- Score

131. How can we incorporate support to ensure safe and effective use of SQL Server Reporting Services into the services that we provide?
<--- Score

132. What knowledge, skills and characteristics mark a good SQL Server Reporting Services project manager?
<--- Score

133. What are your most important goals for the strategic SQL Server Reporting Services objectives?
<--- Score

134. What one word do we want to own in the minds of our customers, employees, and partners?
<--- Score

135. Will there be any necessary staff changes (redundancies or new hires)?
<--- Score

136. What have we done to protect our business from competitive encroachment?
<--- Score

137. How will we insure seamless interoperability of SQL Server Reporting Services moving forward?
<--- Score

138. Have totally satisfied customers?
<--- Score

139. How will we build a 100-year startup?
<--- Score

140. What are the success criteria that will indicate that SQL Server Reporting Services objectives have been met and the benefits delivered?
<--- Score

141. How does SQL Server Reporting Services integrate with other business initiatives?
<--- Score

142. How will we know when our strategy has been successful?
<--- Score

143. What are your key business, operational, societal responsibility, and human resource strategic challenges and advantages?
<--- Score

144. Am I failing differently each time?
<--- Score

145. If we got kicked out and the board brought in a new CEO, what would he do?
<--- Score

146. Do we have enough freaky customers in our portfolio pushing us to the limit day in and day out?
<--- Score

147. Are we changing as fast as the world around us?
<--- Score

148. How much does SQL Server Reporting Services help?

<--- Score

149. Who is responsible for ensuring appropriate resources (time, people and money) are allocated to SQL Server Reporting Services?

<--- Score

150. What is the purpose of SQL Server Reporting Services in relation to the mission?

<--- Score

151. What is the overall business strategy?

<--- Score

152. Do we underestimate the customer's journey?

<--- Score

153. What are the Essentials of Internal SQL Server Reporting Services Management?

<--- Score

154. Ask yourself: how would we do this work if we only had one staff member to do it?

<--- Score

155. Instead of going to current contacts for new ideas, what if you reconnected with dormant contacts--the people you used to know? If you were going reactivate a dormant tie, who would it be?

<--- Score

156. What are the rules and assumptions my industry operates under? What if the opposite were true?

<--- Score

157. Who will determine interim and final deadlines?

<--- Score

158. What potential megatrends could make our business model obsolete?

<--- Score

159. What are strategies for increasing support and reducing opposition?

<--- Score

160. How do I stay inspired?

<--- Score

161. What may be the consequences for the performance of an organization if all stakeholders are not consulted regarding SQL Server Reporting Services?

<--- Score

162. If there were zero limitations, what would we do differently?

<--- Score

163. Who is responsible for errors?

<--- Score

164. How can we become more high-tech but still be high touch?

<--- Score

165. What are the long-term SQL Server Reporting Services goals?

<--- Score

166. How is business? Why?
<--- Score

167. What are internal and external SQL Server Reporting Services relations?
<--- Score

168. Do SQL Server Reporting Services rules make a reasonable demand on a users capabilities?
<--- Score

169. Who will provide the final approval of SQL Server Reporting Services deliverables?
<--- Score

170. Who do we think the world wants us to be?
<--- Score

171. If our company went out of business tomorrow, would anyone who doesn't get a paycheck here care?
<--- Score

172. How do you listen to customers to obtain actionable information?
<--- Score

173. Operational - will it work?
<--- Score

174. Whom among your colleagues do you trust, and for what?
<--- Score

175. Would you rather sell to knowledgeable and informed customers or to uninformed customers?

<--- Score

176. Who uses our product in ways we never expected?
<--- Score

177. What should we stop doing?
<--- Score

178. Who have we, as a company, historically been when we've been at our best?
<--- Score

179. But does it really, really work?
<--- Score

180. What is the estimated value of the project?
<--- Score

181. Is SQL Server Reporting Services dependent on the successful delivery of a current project?
<--- Score

182. How will you know that the SQL Server Reporting Services project has been successful?
<--- Score

183. What is it like to work for me?
<--- Score

184. If our customer were my grandmother, would I tell her to buy what we're selling?
<--- Score

185. What is Effective SQL Server Reporting Services?
<--- Score

186. What does your signature ensure?
<--- Score

187. To whom do you add value?
<--- Score

188. What is your BATNA (best alternative to a negotiated agreement)?
<--- Score

189. Who else should we help?
<--- Score

190. What are your organizations work systems?
<--- Score

191. Is there a lack of internal resources to do this work?
<--- Score

192. Who will use it?
<--- Score

193. What is the funding source for this project?
<--- Score

194. What sources do you use to gather information for a SQL Server Reporting Services study?
<--- Score

195. If I had to leave my organization for a year and the only communication I could have with employees was a single paragraph, what would I write?
<--- Score

196. What are the usability implications of SQL Server Reporting Services actions?
<--- Score

197. Who is the main stakeholder, with ultimate responsibility for driving SQL Server Reporting Services forward?
<--- Score

198. What kind of crime could a potential new hire have committed that would not only not disqualify him/her from being hired by our organization, but would actually indicate that he/she might be a particularly good fit?
<--- Score

199. What was the last experiment we ran?
<--- Score

200. How to Secure SQL Server Reporting Services?
<--- Score

201. Are new benefits received and understood?
<--- Score

202. What happens if you do not have enough funding?
<--- Score

203. What is our formula for success in SQL Server Reporting Services ?
<--- Score

204. Which functions and people interact with the supplier and or customer?

<--- Score

205. Is a SQL Server Reporting Services Team Work effort in place?
<--- Score

206. Did my employees make progress today?
<--- Score

207. How do senior leaders set organizational vision and values?
<--- Score

208. Is the SQL Server Reporting Services organization completing tasks effectively and efficiently?
<--- Score

209. What would I recommend my friend do if he were facing this dilemma?
<--- Score

210. If no one would ever find out about my accomplishments, how would I lead differently?
<--- Score

211. Where is your organization on the performance excellence continuum?
<--- Score

212. What is the craziest thing we can do?
<--- Score

213. What happens when a new employee joins the organization?
<--- Score

214. Has implementation been effective in reaching specified objectives?

<--- Score

215. Do your leaders set clear a direction that is aligned with the vision, mission, and values and is cascaded throughout the organization with measurable goals?

<--- Score

216. Is it economical; do we have the time and money?

<--- Score

217. Are we making progress? and are we making progress as SQL Server Reporting Services leaders?

<--- Score

218. Where is our petri dish?

<--- Score

219. Which individuals, teams or departments will be involved in SQL Server Reporting Services?

<--- Score

220. In a project to restructure SQL Server Reporting Services outcomes, which stakeholders would you involve?

<--- Score

221. Which SQL Server Reporting Services goals are the most important?

<--- Score

222. How are conflicts dealt with?
<--- Score

223. How do we go about Securing SQL Server Reporting Services?
<--- Score

224. How are we doing compared to our industry?
<--- Score

225. What is an unauthorized commitment?
<--- Score

226. What is a feasible sequencing of reform initiatives over time?
<--- Score

227. Do you have a vision statement?
<--- Score

228. Think of your SQL Server Reporting Services project. what are the main functions?
<--- Score

229. What is our SQL Server Reporting Services Strategy?
<--- Score

230. Are the assumptions believable and achievable?
<--- Score

231. Are there any disadvantages to implementing SQL Server Reporting Services? There might be some that are less obvious?
<--- Score

232. How do we provide a safe environment -physically and emotionally?
<--- Score

Add up total points for this section:
_ _ _ _ _ = Total points for this section

Divided by: _ _ _ _ _ _ (number of
statements answered) = _ _ _ _ _ _
Average score for this section

Transfer your score to the SQL Server
Reporting Services Index at the
beginning of the Self-Assessment.

Index

CPSIA information can be obtained
at www.ICGtesting.com
Printed in the USA
LVHW052215021219
639233LV00017B/634/P